Contents

To Our Readers

We thought about creating this book for the Who HQ series for a long time and decided, in light of the COVID-19 pandemic, that it was a very necessary one to include, especially now. The AIDS crisis is a grim subject that deals with a terrible disease and the US government's indifference to it. But *What Is the AIDS Crisis?* also chronicles an uplifting moment in history when the gay community courageously fought to be seen and heard during a time of prejudice and fear.

Our series is no stranger to tackling difficult topics. We believe that Who HQ is a destination for readers, families, teachers, and librarians seeking to learn about the complex world that we share.

The AIDS crisis is far from over, and its origins are sad and dark. We have worked hard to tell this story in a way that will be educational and meaningful to all our readers.

We hope this book is one that enlightens many.

Francesco Sedita

Francesco Sedita
Publisher, Who HQ

As an HIV activist for most of my career, I have been fortunate to work with many people who fought on the front lines of the epidemic in the 1980s and 1990s. Yet for so many young people, much of that history has been lost along with the lives taken by the disease.

What Is the AIDS Crisis? preserves that history. The story of the HIV/AIDS epidemic is about a community rising up to fight a deadly virus, challenging the most powerful people in the world, and channeling their suffering into making the world a better place. The activists in ACT UP and other organizations are the reason millions of people's lives have been saved.

The HIV/AIDS epidemic is not over. Nearly one million people die from HIV around the world each year, and many cannot access the treatment and prevention they need to tackle this disease. Activism is as important now as ever to end the HIV/AIDS epidemic once and for all.

Christian Antonio Urrutia
Cofounder, PrEP4All

PrEP4All fights to ensure that everyone, everywhere, can access the HIV medications they need.

What Is the AIDS Crisis?

October 11, 1987—Washington, DC

As the sun rose over the nation's capital, people gathered along the National Mall, the lawn stretching from the Lincoln Memorial to the US Capitol building. They were there to honor the friends and loved ones they had lost to an illness called AIDS. Since 1980, the disease had taken the lives of more than twenty thousand Americans. In 1987 alone, 16,488 more would die.

In memory of the dead, an enormous quilt had been made. Each of the quilt's 1,920 panels measured three feet across and six feet tall—about the size of a grave. Every piece of fabric—sewn, printed, embroidered, or hand-painted—was dedicated to a person who had died. A child. A friend. A parent.

As teams of volunteers unfurled the quilt, the names of the dead were read aloud. Some people remained silent. Some cried. Many hugged one another. News crews broadcast the event to millions of Americans watching on TV.

Actor Whoopi Goldberg read out some of the names. "I've lost sixty of my friends to AIDS," she told the *New York Times*. "I'm here for me, my friends, my daughter, and all of those who are suffering."

This was the first public appearance of the AIDS Memorial Quilt. At this time, it was larger than a football field. But it would keep growing as more died.

Most of the victims of the AIDS crisis were gay men. But seven years into the epidemic, the disease was spreading to more Americans than ever before. (*Epidemic* is when an infectious disease becomes widespread within a community. *Pandemic* is an epidemic that has spread worldwide.)

"Too much of the sorrow is confined to one group of Americans," one gay man said, "and I think the rest of America needs to be aware of what's going on here."

After the display of the AIDS Memorial Quilt, a march began. As many as three hundred thousand took part.

There would be more marches on Washington. Darker days and much more death lay ahead.

The story of the AIDS crisis is one of fear. Fear of a strange new disease and a terrifying, painful death.

It is also a story of hope and people banding together to take care of—and fight for—one another. To make the US government face the crisis and finally do something about it.

And it is a story of science and discovery—of fighting to outsmart an invisible virus.

What Is HIV/AIDS?

HIV is a virus that, when left untreated, can lead to AIDS. HIV, which stands for "human immunodeficiency virus," is spread through blood or certain sexual contact. It can also pass from an infected pregnant

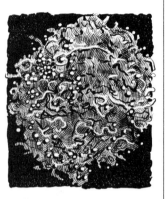

A cell infected with HIV

woman to her unborn child. (It is *not* passed through the air or by hugging or kissing.)

HIV attacks the immune system, the body's natural defense against disease and infection. *AIDS* stands for "acquired immunodeficiency syndrome." AIDS can occur when an HIV infection is untreated. The immune system is so damaged, it can no longer fight infection. For someone with full-blown AIDS, even catching a cold can become fatal.

CHAPTER 1
The First to Fall

In the fall of 1979, a fifth-grade teacher in New York City named Rick Wellikoff noticed strange bumps behind his ear. He visited a doctor and found out he had Kaposi's sarcoma, a rare skin cancer. "KS" usually affected men in their fifties and sixties, not someone in their midthirties, like Rick.

Throughout the next year, 1980, Rick felt exhausted. He had to quit his job. That summer, instead of a vacation, he stayed home to rest.

Nick Rock was a handsome young man who worked on a cruise ship. That same summer, he joined friends at their beach house on Fire Island, near New York City. But Nick wasn't his usual fun-loving self.

Like Rick, Nick was always tired. And he was sick to his stomach and losing a lot of weight. He, too, could no longer work. He had visited doctor after doctor, but his health only worsened. Nick's boyfriend, Enno Poersch, hoped some fresh ocean air would do Nick good.

But by September, back in New York City, Nick was so weak, he could barely move. Sitting up in bed and getting dressed could take an hour. His body began to change. His back and shoulders hunched over.

On Halloween night, Nick fell unconscious. Enno rushed him to the hospital, where X-rays revealed three lesions on Nick's brain. (*Lesions* are areas of damaged tissue that are caused by injury or disease.) Doctors thought he had a disease commonly found in cats. Thanks to the body's immune system, most people exposed to this disease recovered quickly . . . but not Nick.

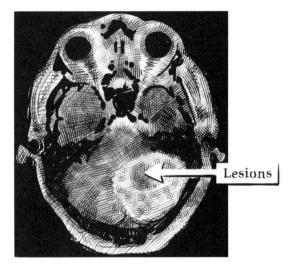

Lesions

Meanwhile, in San Francisco, California, Ken Horne—a thirty-seven-year-old gay man and former ballet dancer—had developed purplish-

blue spots across his body. "My life is falling apart," he told his doctor. Ken had also felt really tired for the past two years.

In New York, Rick Wellikoff's health took a turn for the worse. His lungs were filling with fluid. In the hospital, a tube was inserted into Rick's chest to help him breathe. But Rick decided he wanted to leave the hospital. To live like this was hardly living at all. His doctors removed the tube, and Rick returned home with his boyfriend. By morning, Rick had died. It was December 24, 1980.

As for Nick Rock, for a short while, his health seemed to be improving. But he had a heart attack and was rushed to the hospital. Nick's body was riddled with infections.

Sometimes Nick would open his eyes, but he couldn't speak. His sister and boyfriend, Enno, were heartbroken. They decided to turn off Nick's breathing machine. Moments later, Nick was gone.

Back in San Francisco, Ken Horne's doctors could find no clear answers for why he kept getting sicker. By November 1981, Ken had lost sight in one eye, and his once-strong dancer's body weighed just 122 pounds. He died on November 30.

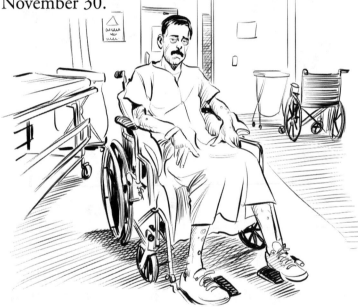

On June 5, 1981, the Centers for Disease Control published an important report. (The CDC is the government agency in charge of protecting Americans from public-health threats.)

The CDC's report was about five young men in Los Angeles who had been treated for a rare form of pneumonia (say: new-MOE-nee-uh), an infection of the lungs. The patients also suffered from other infections.

By the time the report was published, all five men were dead.

The report noted a strange coincidence: All the patients were gay.

These men in Los Angeles—along with Rick Wellikoff, Nick Rock, and Ken Horne—were among the first known Americans to die of AIDS.

More deaths quickly followed. There were 466 in 1982. Ten years later, in 1992, there were more than *forty thousand*.

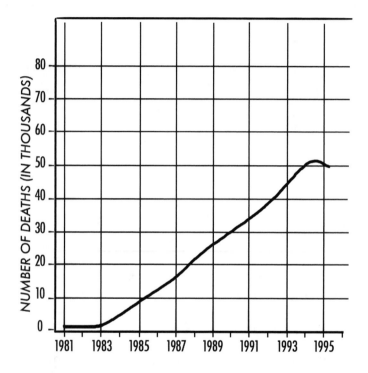

In the frightening early days of this health crisis, the disease didn't even have a name. No one understood what was killing these young gay men.

CHAPTER 2
"Gay Cancer"

The CDC study caught the attention of Dr. Alvin Friedman-Kien in New York City. He phoned the CDC to report that he and some other doctors had been treating a group of patients for KS, the rare skin cancer. Just like the patients from the CDC report, these KS patients were all gay men.

Dr. Alvin Friedman-Kien

More calls came in to the CDC from doctors around the country about patients—all gay— who were sick and dying from KS and PCP (the rare pneumonia). Whatever was causing these gay men to fall ill was clearly a widespread problem. The CDC formed a group to study and learn more.

In July 1981, the *Bay Area Reporter*, a gay and lesbian community paper in San Francisco, ran a short article about "'Gay Men's' Pneumonia." It encouraged gay men experiencing shortness of breath to visit their doctors.

Days later, the *New York Times* ran an article about KS under the headline "Rare Cancer Seen in 41 Homosexuals." (*Homosexual* is a word used to describe a gay person, but the term is considered aggressive and offensive today.) Many of the patients went to gay clubs and used certain drugs. The doctors wondered if the drugs could be responsible for the disease. The article suggested it was unlikely the disease was spread from person to person. One doctor pointed out that "no cases have been reported . . . outside the homosexual community or in women."

This would not be the case for long.

People began referring to the disease that had no name as "gay cancer." Scientists even briefly called it gay-related immune deficiency (GRID). The fact that the disease was described this way only resulted in harmful misunderstandings about AIDS for years to come.

What Does It Mean to Be LGBTQ+ (Lesbian, Gay, Bisexual, Transgender, Queer, Plus)?

Love and *identity*—what makes someone who they are—take many forms:

Lesbian: a woman whose physical, romantic, and emotional attractions are to other women. The word *lesbian* comes from the Greek island of Lesbos, where the female poet Sappho lived and wrote about the beauty of women.

Gay: people whose attraction is to people of the same sex.

Bisexual: someone whose attractions are to people of the same or opposite sex, or different genders.

Transgender: people whose *gender* (how they feel on the inside, and how they express themselves) is different from the *sex* (male or female) they were assigned at birth. Some trans people decide to undergo surgery or other medical treatment so their outward appearance matches their true self.

Queer: once considered an offensive term, some people have reclaimed it to refer to any identity that is not strictly heterosexual (people attracted to people of the opposite sex). Some queer people prefer to be called "they" instead of "he" or "she."

(*+/Plus*): people who don't feel that any of these categories fully describe them.

In 2020, 5.6 percent of American adults—an estimated eighteen million people—identified as LGBTQ+.

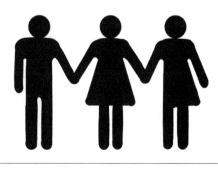

Yes, in those early days of the crisis, it was gay men who were most affected. And since few others besides doctors and nurses were helping them, it was the queer community that rose up to fight the disease and care for the sick.

CASES OF GAY-RELATED IMMUNE DEFICIENCY

CHAPTER 3
Community

On August 11, 1981, a famous writer named Larry Kramer hosted a gathering of eighty gay men at his New York City apartment to discuss what was happening. Among Larry's guests that night was Enno Poersch, the boyfriend of Nick Rock,

Larry Kramer

who had died barely six months earlier.

Larry, who was also gay, invited Dr. Alvin Friedman-Kien to present the facts on this so-called gay cancer.

"We're only seeing the tip of the iceberg,"

the doctor said. Many more cases—and more deaths—were sure to come. Money was needed to study the disease. But getting any money from the government would take too long. Larry and his guests contributed $6,635 that night to help pay Dr. Friedman-Kien to start research.

Larry and his friends thought they could raise much more money on Fire Island on Labor Day weekend. The vacation spot was popular with the New York City gay community.

They printed and distributed thousands of copies of a news article about the health crisis and gave information about how to donate to Dr. Friedman-Kien's research. Unfortunately, among fifteen thousand gay men, only $124 was raised.

In the months that followed, major newspapers barely covered the story. Larry Kramer made calls to the mayor's office, trying to alert him to the unfolding crisis. Those calls were not returned. "If KS were a new form of cancer attacking straight people," Larry wrote, "it would

President Ronald Reagan

be receiving constant media attention." No help came, either, from newly elected President Ronald Reagan and his administration.

Either few people realized how serious the situation was—or worse, they didn't care.

In October 1981, a San Francisco nurse named Bobbi Campbell learned he had KS. Bobbi wanted to spread awareness about the disease. So he became the first person to speak of his KS publicly. He took Polaroid photos of his purple skin lesions and created posters of himself. He urged people to take the disease seriously. The posters were taped in the windows of a pharmacy in the Castro, the city's gay neighborhood.

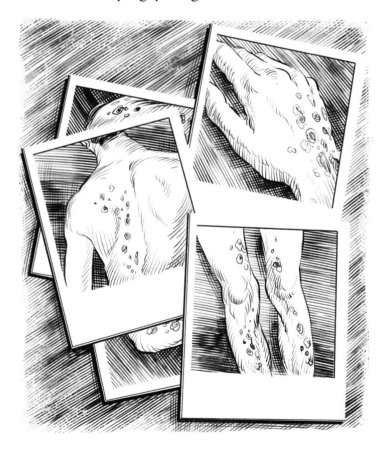

He called himself the "KS Poster Boy." By December, Bobbi was writing about his experience in the local gay paper. He called his column the "Gay Cancer Journal."

Bobbi started a support group at the city's new KS clinic. It was sponsored by the Shanti Project.

The Shanti Project connected terminally ill cancer patients with volunteers offering them comfort and help. (Not all people have someone close to them to be there at the end of their life.)

Some who fell ill were fired from their jobs. Others had uncaring landlords who kicked them out of their homes. Shanti provided housing for some of these patients. As more people got sick, more volunteers joined the Shanti Project.

A support group organized by the Shanti Project

Back in New York, on January 4, 1982, Larry Kramer—along with five other men—established the Gay Men's Health Crisis (GMHC). Without help from the government, "[they] were forced to take care of [them]selves," said one of the GMHC's first volunteers.

Gay men, lesbians, and straight supporters of the queer community—doctors, lawyers, artists, many kinds of people—came together at the GMHC. Volunteers did everyday chores for sick people like cooking, cleaning, shopping, and caring for pets. One GMHC volunteer set up a telephone hotline—the first of its kind— where people could leave a message on his home answering machine. The hotline received more than one hundred phone calls on its first night.

Meanwhile, the CDC task force and other scientists continued to study the disease using what little money they had. Still, requests for more government funding were largely ignored.

New cases also appeared in people who were not gay. At first, it was mainly intravenous drug users and the babies they gave birth to. (*Intravenous* means "in the veins." Some illegal drugs are injected into the veins using needles. If those needles are shared, the disease can be passed along.) Hemophiliacs— people with a blood disorder that requires transfers of other people's blood—were also contracting the disease.

By September 1982, the CDC had finally given the disease its name: acquired immune deficiency syndrome. AIDS.

CHAPTER 4
Liberation

In 1982, the CDC reported that AIDS could be caught through sexual contact. For many in the gay community, this came as particularly disturbing news. To understand why, one must look back at gay life in America over the previous thirty years.

In the 1950s, gay behavior was illegal practically everywhere in the United States. There wasn't much sense of community among gay people. That's because most led secret, closeted lives. *Closeted* means a person is not telling others they are gay. If a person was "out"—living openly as gay—their friends or family might stop seeing them. They might be fired from their job.

In the 1960s, some of the few places gay people could meet one another, and be at ease among people like themselves, were bars that welcomed gay people. Most often, these "gay bars" were found in big cities. Still, there were laws forbidding same-sex couples from dancing together. So gay bars were often raided by the police. Customers were called names, beaten, and arrested.

One hot June night in 1969, the Stonewall Inn—a popular gay bar in New York City—was raided by the police . . . and the people inside

fought back. Bottles, bricks, and punches were thrown. Riot police were called in to restore order. Word spread fast, and queer people poured into the area from all across the city—gay men, lesbians, and trans people alike—to take the fight to the streets. No one was killed, and after a few nights of tense confrontations, the cops backed down.

After Stonewall, queer life changed in America. Throughout the 1970s, a new "out and proud" queer community grew. They worked to change laws and fight for equal rights. Gay pride parades and parties are still held every year to remember Stonewall and to celebrate gay liberation.

During this time, thousands of people came out of the closet. They flocked to gay-friendly neighborhoods like the Castro in San Francisco and Greenwich Village in New York. They made friends, formed new queer families, and established gay-friendly communities.

The Castro

To be gay and liberated meant freedom to love whom you wanted. For many—gay and straight people alike—this time of "free love" meant having many sexual partners. People often met in gyms, bars, and clubs. They danced all night to the sound of the 1970s, disco. And they felt freer than ever before. But this freedom came with risks—many risks.

Although no one knew it at the time, HIV had been quietly spreading from person to person in New York City since the early 1970s. Scientists later learned that HIV/AIDS has a long "latency" period. That meant that before a person showed signs of illness, they already had been infected—and possibly spreading it to others—for years. The disease reached San Francisco in 1976. By the early 1980s, roughly half of the gay men in the city were infected.

Learning that AIDS could be spread through sexual contact worried the gay community. Freedom meant so much to queer people. And many doctors were not trusted. This was in part because, for decades, doctors said being gay was a mental illness that could be "cured" through horrible methods like electroshock therapy and lobotomies, a kind of brain surgery. These "treatments" could result in brain damage or even death. (It was not until 1973 that the American Psychiatric Association stopped considering being gay a mental illness.)

Before reliable HIV tests became widely available in 1985, many feared they had the disease but didn't know it—and that it was only a matter of time before they fell ill. It was like a sword over their heads, waiting to fall.

Where Did HIV/AIDS Come From?

The first case of HIV likely occurred around 1908, in the jungles of southeast Cameroon, a country in central Africa. The virus passed to a human hunter from a chimpanzee, through its meat or blood. From there, an infected traveler took the virus downriver to Kinshasa, now the capital of the Democratic

Republic of the Congo (DRC). When the DRC became independent in 1960, doctors, nurses, and lawyers from the Caribbean nation of Haiti traveled there to lend a helping hand. The virus reached Haiti around 1967, then the United States soon after. Robert Rayford, a Black teenager who died in St. Louis, Missouri, in 1969, was likely the first American to die of AIDS.

CHAPTER 5
Living and Dying in Dignity

People in the gay community on both sides of the country continued to spread news about AIDS—and, most importantly, how to prevent HIV.

In November 1982, Michael Callen and Richard Berkowitz—two gay New Yorkers living with AIDS—wrote to a local gay newspaper,

Michael Callen and Richard Berkowitz writing
their letter to the gay community

pleading with their community to take AIDS seriously. "We know who we are, and we know why we're sick," they wrote. "The party that was the '70s is over."

Michael and Richard—along with a medical expert—created a forty-page booklet about how to prevent the spread of HIV/AIDS. The booklet said "safe sex"—namely, the use of condoms—could greatly reduce the risk of getting AIDS.

When new information became available, the booklet was updated, reprinted, and distributed nationwide.

In San Francisco, the Sisters of Perpetual Indulgence—a drag-queen activist group that included "KS Poster Boy" Bobbi Campbell—published their own pamphlet. (A drag queen is a person, usually a man, who dresses and performs as a woman—the Sisters dressed as nuns.) Titled *Play Fair!*, the Sisters' pamphlet contained much of the same information as the New York booklet.

Bobbi and the Sisters

The rainbow flag

Ryan White, attending school in 1987

ACT UP protesters gather at the White House during
Ronald Reagan's presidency.

Writer and activist Larry Kramer, cofounder of Gay Men's Health Crisis

San Francisco nurse Bobbi Campbell

The Sisters of Perpetual Indulgence in San Francisco, 1980

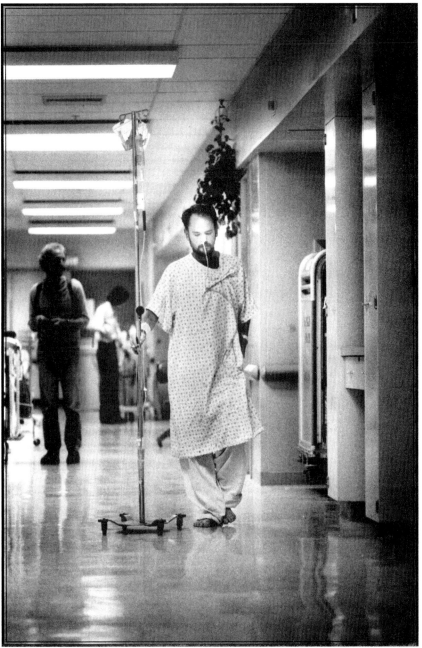

An AIDS patient in San Francisco General Hospital, 1984

THE FIRST AIDS WARD

On July 25, 1983,

here on Ward 5B, a group of caregivers gathered to confront

a new epidemic: AIDS. They created a haven of acceptance

and compassion at a time when others called for isolation and rejection.

They saw fellow human beings where others saw only contagion and disease.

With the volunteer participation of a generous, loving community, they

developed an internationally-renowned center of excellence committed

to quality of care for the living and the dying. This plaque

commemorates all who served here and remembers all who died.

July 2003

A plaque in San Francisco General Hospital
honors the first ever AIDS ward.

Marchers at the Lesbian and Gay Pride March in New York City in 1983

Actor Rock Hudson

amfAR's first chairperson, Elizabeth Taylor, speaks at a fundraiser in 1990.

AIDS activists at an ACT UP meeting in New York City in 1990

Members of ACT UP protest near the White House in 1992.

The Gay Men's Health Crisis takes part in
New York City's 2019 Pride March.

Part of the AIDS Memorial Quilt displayed in Washington, DC

Ronald Reagan (far left) and members of the Presidential Commission
on the HIV Epidemic in 1987

A protester carries a "Silence = Death" poster.

In 1985, a parent and her two children protest
those with AIDS being allowed to go to school.

Parents protest against people with AIDS
going to school with their children. .

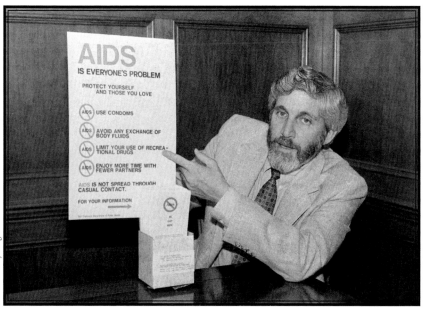

Dr. Mervyn F. Silverman attempts to educate the
public on how to reduce the spread of HIV.

Volunteers at the AIDS hotline

Nearly two thousand people participate
in a candlelight parade in San Francisco, 1983

In the days before the Internet—before most households even owned a personal computer—these printed publications provided people with lifesaving information.

However, without a cure, doctors and nurses could treat only symptoms. They prescribed experimental medicines to try to extend patients' lives. In some cases, the treatments felt worse than the disease. One patient said that for days after taking the drugs, he felt like he'd been run over by a truck. Still, many would do anything to survive for as long as they could.

The CDC still did not understand much about HIV/AIDS. It did not confirm until

September 1983 that HIV *could not be spread* through the air, through saliva, or on surfaces. Some doctors and nurses refused to treat, or even touch, AIDS patients. Most insurance companies denied health-care coverage to people with AIDS.

At San Francisco General Hospital, one nurse remembered: "There would be patients with three meal trays stacked up outside the room, because people were too afraid to go [into the room to deliver it]."

In order to improve care, San Francisco General Hospital opened the world's first clinic for AIDS patients in 1983. The clinic worked with the Shanti Project and other groups. Visitors could stay overnight, even if they weren't blood relatives or married. (Same-sex marriage would not be legal nationwide until 2015.)

Patients were cared for in "Ward 5B" by brave, dedicated nurses and doctors who had volunteered for the job. Many were lesbians and saw the patients as members of their community—their gay brothers.

Nurses who worked in Ward 5B

Unlike some nurses and doctors at the time, those in Ward 5B were unafraid to touch, hug,

and care for their patients. Head nurse Alison Moed told the *New York Times*: "There is such a sense of love and basic human sharing here. It's a place where a disease has brought out the best in people."

Volunteers visited regularly to lift people's spirits. Every Sunday for eighteen years, Rita

Rockett and her friends brought meals and entertainment to the patients. They called themselves "the Brunch Bunch." Rita, who worked as a travel agent during the week, was much beloved for her joy-filled performances. "To be a positive light in the darkness," Rita said. "That's all I wanted to do."

Rita Rockett performs

The AIDS ward at San Francisco General became a model for the rest of the world in how to treat HIV/AIDS patients. St. Vincent's Hospital in New York City soon opened its own AIDS ward.

Also in 1983, Congress finally provided some federal funding for AIDS research and treatment: just $12 million.

Three AIDS activists speaking to Congress

Attendees at the Gay and Lesbian Health Conference
in Denver, Colorado

By then, AIDS cases had been reported in more than thirty states. But most of the activist groups were in the big cities like New York, San Francisco, and Los Angeles. That all changed in June at the Gay and Lesbian Health Conference in Denver, Colorado, when the movement became truly national.

The AIDS Walk

In 1986, the Gay Men's Health Crisis (GMHC) held its first annual AIDS Walk in New York City. It was a way for all kinds of people—queer and straight, young and old, ordinary and famous—to help the cause. That first year, more than $700,000 was raised by 4,500 walkers.

Soon, more cities began to hold their own walks. Many people who walked wore red ribbons, which became a symbol of the fight against AIDS in 1991. By its thirty-fifth year, the AIDS Walk had raised more than $150 million and nearly 900,000 walkers had participated.

Among those in attendance were Bobbi Campbell, Michael Callen, and Richard Berkowitz—three of the men responsible for the informative safe-sex booklets. They joined with eight other gay men living with AIDS to form a national association. They named their organization People with AIDS. At the conference, eleven articles (points) were read aloud. They became known as the Denver Principles.

The Denver Principles rejected the labels of "victims" or "patients." Instead, they say: "People with AIDS (PWAs)." They said PWAs should  not be blamed for their condition. PWAs must be involved in all decisions on health policy and for their own care. PWAs deserved quality health care, free of discrimination. The last of the eleven points declared that PWAs deserved "to die—and to LIVE—in dignity."

The fight against AIDS—and the fight to care for and protect PWAs—had gone nationwide. From apartments to community centers, from hospital wards to conference halls, people were taking action.

But the road ahead would be long and difficult.

CHAPTER 6
Stigma

By 1984, scientists had discovered what would become known as HIV, the virus that can lead to full-blown AIDS. The next year, blood tests were developed to detect HIV.

This was important progress. Yet the United States government still had no real nationwide response to the fast-spreading epidemic. Information was not provided to the public in a clear or honest way.

Consequently, as more Americans became aware of HIV/AIDS, *mis*information spread.

Since HIV/AIDS had been thought of as "gay cancer" from the beginning, fear and mistrust of gay people grew.

Some people thought they could "catch" AIDS from a gay man coughing next to them on a bus. Or from a gay waiter serving them at a restaurant. Or at a public pool or from a toilet seat. What about from a mosquito bite? Or a hug or a handshake?

These fears were not based in fact.

Sometimes, fear comes from hatred. In 1983, Pat Buchanan, President Reagan's director of communications, called AIDS "nature's revenge on gay men." Reverend Jerry Falwell called it "God's punishment for the society that tolerates homosexuals." One man speaking at a political conference in 1985 suggested one solution might be the "extermination"—the killing—of gay people.

Hate crimes against gay men and lesbians rose sharply during this time. Twenty states tried to pass laws that would ban PWAs from certain jobs, like teaching. Some states would make it a crime to transmit HIV to another person. Some of these proposals actually became law.

Having HIV/AIDS became a stigma—a mark of shame. PWAs became *stigmatized* as if they weren't good people and that's why they got sick. As if it were their fault.

It was not just gay men with AIDS who lived with the stigma.

Ryan White was a thirteen-year-old student in Indiana. He had hemophilia and contracted AIDS in 1984 after receiving a blood transfusion that contained the virus. Ryan became terribly ill and was told by doctors he had just six months to live. But Ryan fought hard to get better, and soon, he felt good enough to return to classes for the 1985–86 school year.

However, Ryan was not welcome back at school.

More than one hundred parents and fifty teachers at Ryan White's school demanded he be kept from attending classes. The principal agreed.

Ryan White

HIV in Blood Banks

Since the 1940s, American "blood banks" have stored human blood for many uses. The United States also supplies other countries with blood. Even when it became clear that HIV could be transmitted through blood, America's blood banks did nothing to find out if their blood supply was okay. No new rules came from the government, either. In 1983, the CDC stepped in. Blood donations could no longer come from high-risk groups, including gay men and intravenous drug users. Testing for HIV became available in 1985. By 1990, however, the CDC determined that nearly five thousand Americans—and many more around the world—had contracted HIV/AIDS from infected blood.

Ryan and his family brought the case to court. They were threatened with violence. People called Ryan terrible names because he had AIDS.

But Ryan also received thousands of letters of support from around the world. His mom told him, "Don't give up, be proud of who you are, and never feel sorry for yourself."

In February, Ryan was finally allowed back in school. But on his first day, almost half the students stayed home. That afternoon, a judge ruled that Ryan had to stay home after all.

In April, Ryan returned to school for good. But he wasn't allowed to take gym class. He couldn't use the same restroom as the other boys. At lunch, Ryan ate with disposable utensils, so cafeteria workers wouldn't have to wash forks and spoons that he had used.

The threats continued. After a bullet was fired into their living-room window, the White family decided to move. Ryan would start high school in a brand-new town. Luckily, the difference between his old and new school was like night and day.

On Ryan's first day, just two of the school's 620 students stayed home. Instead of threats and name-calling, Ryan was greeted in the hallways with handshakes.

The credit for the warm welcome Ryan received on his first day of high school belongs in great part to a student named Jill Stewart. She was the student-body president. Before Ryan started, Jill had invited medical experts to talk to her classmates about HIV/AIDS. At home, the students shared what they'd learned with their families.

Jill was proof that one person can truly make a difference. Amazingly, a high-school student was doing a better job than the government at educating Americans about HIV/AIDS. Ryan, like so many PWAs, had to fight not only to stay alive, but he also had to battle people's fear and ignorance just to go to school like other kids.

Over the next few years, Ryan appeared on popular television shows and the cover of *People* magazine.

He traveled to classrooms around the country, educating people young and old about AIDS. He wrote a book about his life. A movie called *The Ryan White Story* aired on ABC.

Ryan lived with AIDS for six years, even though doctors had said he would die in six months. In April 1990, just a month before his graduation from high school, Ryan White died from the disease.

Four months later, Congress passed the Ryan White Comprehensive AIDS Resources Emergency (CARE) Act, which provided money for the treatment of people living with AIDS. What an honor to Ryan's memory.

CHAPTER 7
Understanding

It took until September 1985 for President Reagan to finally mention AIDS in public. What made him do it? Perhaps because earlier that year, one of Reagan's friends had announced that he was gay and dying of AIDS. That man was a famous Hollywood actor named Rock Hudson.

Rock Hudson

Speaking at a White House press conference, President Reagan claimed that AIDS research had been one of his "top priorities." (The year before, however, when asked by a reporter if the president was worried about the spread of AIDS, Reagan's press secretary had replied, "I haven't heard him express concern.")

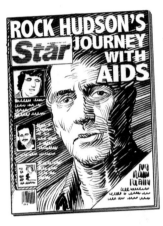

Americans followed Rock Hudson's story closely. Over the next six months, the number of stories about HIV/AIDS in major newspapers and magazines more than tripled.

In October, Rock Hudson passed away at the age of fifty-nine. He was one of nearly seven thousand Americans to die from AIDS in 1985 alone.

In his will, Rock left $250,000 to help establish the American Foundation for AIDS Research (amfAR). His close friend, Hollywood actor Elizabeth Taylor, served as amfAR's first chairperson. Singer Dionne Warwick—along with Stevie Wonder, Elton John, and Gladys Knight—recorded a version of the hit song "That's What Friends Are For" to raise money for amfAR.

Gladys Knight, Dionne Warwick, Elton John, and Stevie Wonder sing "That's What Friends Are For"

"Understanding AIDS"

In 1986, President Reagan asked Dr. C. Everett Koop, the US Surgeon General, to prepare a report on HIV/AIDS. In the introduction, Dr. Koop wrote: "We are fighting a disease, not people. . . . The country must face this epidemic as a unified society." The report stated that the best way to

Dr. C. Everett Koop

protect against the disease was abstinence—avoiding sexual relations entirely—or monogamy (having sexual relations with only one person). But for the people who did not choose to do either, the report said that safe-sex practices, like using condoms, were necessary. Twenty million copies of this report were distributed to local governments, schools, and doctor's offices across the country.

Two years later, Dr. Koop published an eight-page brochure called "Understanding AIDS." It was made available in eight languages, as well as in Braille and on tape, and it was mailed to all 107 million American households. It was the largest public mailing in history. But was this too little, too late?

In 1986, Jerry Smith, a former tight end for Washington, DC, pro football team, announced  he was dying of AIDS. The six-foot-three athlete had withered away from 210 pounds to 150. Seven weeks later, Jerry Smith died. He was forty-three.

"I want people to know what I've been through and how terrible this disease is," Smith told the *Washington Post*. "Maybe it will help people understand. . . . Maybe something positive will come out of this."

Jerry Smith

That year, President Reagan requested $126 million for AIDS research in the federal budget—ten times more than was spent in 1984. Congress increased this to nearly $190 million.

But would it be enough? Or would AIDS rage on?

CHAPTER 8
Acting Up

For many, the government's response to the AIDS crisis was not viewed as a success. The number of Americans who died of AIDS in 1986 was roughly the same as in the previous six years *combined*.

People in the gay community said they attended more funerals than birthdays during this troubled time. Pride marches became memorials to those who'd passed away. So many were lost, people had to keep lists of their friends and acquaintances who had died. "When that list got to be . . . around a hundred," one man recalled, "I stopped." So many years into the crisis, and the only suggested defense for PWAs was a healthy lifestyle and a brave, hopeful attitude.

Medications were being developed. But the Food and Drug Administration (FDA)—the government agency in charge of approving new drugs for the public—was slow to make the drugs available. Some drug approvals could take ten years!

Larry Kramer, speaking at the Lesbian and Gay Center in New York City in March 1987, said it was time for gay people to get organized, speak out, and *do* something. "I have never been able to understand," he said, "why we have sat back and let ourselves literally be knocked off . . . without fighting back."

Days later, the AIDS Coalition to Unleash Power—ACT UP—was formed. Its members were "united in anger and committed to direct action." ACT UP would stage many protests to challenge drug companies, banks, and the government. Lifesaving AIDS medications had to be developed much faster and provided to anyone who wanted them.

One week after ACT UP's founding, AZT—the first medication for treating AIDS—finally

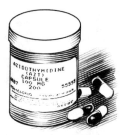

AZT medication

hit the market. Studies had shown that some people who took AZT lived longer than those who did not. Finally, there was reason for hope . . . until people learned of the price tag. Ten thousand dollars, per person, per year. (That would be more than twenty thousand dollars in today's money.) Who could afford this? Particularly when so many PWAs were too sick to work or no longer had health insurance.

On March 24, 1987, ACT UP staged a protest on Wall Street. (Wall Street is a central area for big businesses in New York City.) Protesters linked arms and blocked traffic for hours. They handed out leaflets calling for an end to unjust treatment of PWAs in jobs, housing, and health care. Seventeen protesters—including doctors and nurses—were arrested. News crews captured the action on film.

Soon after ACT UP's first protest, the FDA announced it would speed up its process for approving new AIDS medications. After more protests, the company that produced AZT lowered the drug's annual cost . . . to $6,500. Not nearly cheap enough.

The Wrong Kind of Government Action

In 1987, the Reagan administration announced actions it would take against HIV/AIDS. But it was not the kind of action ACT UP was calling for.

The United States would now ban any foreign travelers living with HIV/AIDS from entering the country. Around the world, the scientific community was shocked. They refused to hold their annual AIDS conference in the United States until the ban was lifted. (The ban would stand for twenty-two years.)

Then, Congress passed a law that prohibited spending federal money on programs that "promoted" either same-sex relations or drug use. This could include educating the public about safe-sex practices, distributing condoms, or setting up "needle exchange" programs that provided clean needles to drug users to prevent them from spreading HIV/AIDS to others.

These policies were not only unhelpful, but they promised to make the crisis worse.

That October, ACT UP joined three hundred thousand people in the nation's capital to demand more action to fight the spread of the disease. "We'll never be silent again!" the protesters chanted. It was there that the AIDS Memorial Quilt was first unveiled.

At the beginning of every Monday-night ACT UP meeting, the names of those who had recently died were read aloud. The meetings ended with a chant: "Act up! Fight back! Fight AIDS!"

The group attracted volunteers from all walks of life, including David Barr, a gay-rights attorney; Ann Northrop, a former TV producer and media expert; Iris Long, a retired chemist; and Peter Staley, a Wall Street bond trader who later quit his job to be a full-time activist.

The AIDS Memorial Quilt

San Francisco activist Cleve Jones founded the NAMES Project AIDS Memorial Quilt in 1987, the same year ACT UP formed in New York. Panels from across the country were mailed to the NAMES Project,

including one for "AIDS Poster Boy" (formerly "KS Poster Boy") Bobbi Campbell, who had died three years earlier. For months, Cleve and his friends sewed them together to create the quilt.

After its unveiling in Washington, DC, the quilt embarked on a twenty-city cross-country tour. The next year, it returned to the capital with more than eight thousand panels. By 1992, it was larger than one hundred football fields. Today, the quilt weighs more than fifty tons and is considered the world's largest community art project.

Within ACT UP, smaller, more focused groups formed, each with specific goals.

Members were taught how to get media attention for their protests. They found ways to appear on TV shows. Other members were trained in how to be arrested without getting hurt. And in the days before cellphone cameras and livestreaming platforms, the "DIVA TV" squad filmed the protests—as well as any police response.

At the weekly meetings, medical experts described the latest scientific findings. They explained how to get new drug treatments and how agencies like the FDA and the National Institutes of Health (NIH) worked.

Over the years, ACT UP grew into an international organization of ten thousand members and 150 local chapters. During the 1988 fifty-city protest called Nine Days of Rage, each day called attention to a different group of people affected by HIV/AIDS: women, people of color, children, prisoners . . .

ACT UP's protests were nonviolent, but they were meant to be disruptive. They were meant to get people's attention and get them thinking.

When the Catholic Church opposed safe-sex education in schools, ACT UP staged a "die-in" at St. Patrick's Cathedral in New York City. Not giving out information about preventing HIV would only lead to more deaths. So protesters lay "dead" in the cathedral's pews and aisles, refusing to get up.

In 1991, when the United States was spending $1 billion a day on the first Gulf War in Iraq, protesters inside Grand Central Station, also in New York City,

tied a banner to a bunch of balloons. It rose to the ceiling. "Money for AIDS, Not for War," the banner read. Later, they held a die-in at then president George H. W. Bush's vacation home in Maine.

ACT UP held its first "political funeral" in 1992, just before the election of President Bill Clinton. Protesters marched from the US Capitol to the White House, carrying the ashes of loved ones who had died. "Bringing the dead to your door!" they chanted. "We won't take it anymore!" Riot police on horseback couldn't stop them from throwing the ashes over the White House fence.

These demonstrations led to progress. After protests at the FDA and the NIH, ACT UP members got to help make decisions with these national health agencies. ACT UP now had a link to the people who could bring new and better medicines to PWAs.

ACT UP members began attending medical conferences and presented their ideas for better ways to treat PWAs. They worked with drug companies and patients to study experimental new drugs.

Still, progress was slow. The drugs were, for the most part, not working. The side effects could be horrible. And more people died every year. ACT UP was doing all it could. Nevertheless, from 1987 through the end of 1992, nearly two hundred thousand lives had been lost to AIDS.

Brothers and sisters; mothers and fathers; aunts, uncles, cousins; friends and lovers. Nearly an entire generation of promising young artists, filmmakers, writers, and musicians, as well as doctors and lawyers, gone too soon. When would the horror and sadness end?

HIV/AIDS on Stage and Screen in the 1990s

Tony Kushner's 1991/1992 play, *Angels in America*, was about AIDS and being gay in 1980s America. The play is full of symbolism and fantasy—some of the characters are ghosts and angels. It won the Tony Award for Best Play as well as the Pulitzer Prize for Drama.

In the 1993 movie *Philadelphia*, Tom Hanks plays a gay man with AIDS who believes he was fired because of his disease and his sexuality. Denzel Washington plays the attorney who represents Hanks's character in court.

Rent is a rock musical based on the 1896 French opera *La Bohème*. It is about a group of struggling young artists living in New York City in the 1990s. Like the characters in the play, the show's creator, Jonathan Larson, had many friends living with HIV/AIDS. *Rent* debuted on Broadway

Rent, the Broadway musical

in 1996 and became a cultural phenomenon, running for twelve years and spawning national tours, a 2005 movie, and a live television special in 2019.

CHAPTER 9
The Cocktail

Since viruses like HIV constantly mutate (change), it's very hard for scientists to destroy them. AZT was the first drug scientists developed to fight HIV/AIDS. But the virus eventually "outsmarted" the drug. AZT didn't work anymore. Because of this, scientists focused on how to *stop* HIV rather than destroy it.

AZT acted on one of the three enzymes inside HIV that help it reproduce. An enzyme is a substance in a living thing that helps start a chemical reaction—or change—inside that living thing.

In 1995, there was a breakthrough. Drugs were developed to act on the *second* of HIV's three important enzymes. A scientific trial was

developed to test whether using two kinds of medications, acting against both enzymes at once, could work against HIV.

Success! Not only did the virus have trouble mutating, but it also could no longer attack the body's immune system. By the end of the year, doctors were prescribing these lifesaving drug combinations. Some started calling the medicines by a nickname: the cocktail.

Within thirty days of taking the pills, HIV levels in some people could no longer be seen! People who had been near death made rapid recoveries.

This was undoubtedly good news, but the daily cocktail also had drawbacks. Early treatments meant taking dozens of pills at very specific times of day. Mess up the schedule, and the virus could come back. The pills also had many bad side effects.

Still, in 1996, for the first time, fewer Americans died from AIDS than had died the previous year. It happened again in 1997, and again the next year, and the next . . .

Finally, the tide had started to turn.

HIV/AIDS in Africa

As AIDS deaths in the United States declined, they increased in Africa. Poorer nations there had little access to testing and health care. By 2002, there were forty million people living with HIV/AIDS around the world. Entire societies were falling apart.

In 2003, President George W. Bush enacted a plan to spend $15 billion, an incredible sum, to treat HIV/AIDS patients in fourteen countries. Finally, in 2007, deaths due to AIDS began to decline. That year, President Bush secured another $30 billion to keep HIV/AIDS on the run.

CHAPTER 10
A Cure?

In 2007, scientists finally disrupted the third enzyme HIV used to reproduce itself. Still, while HIV could be *stopped*, it was not yet *cured*. So researchers next tried to develop drugs to prevent HIV infection from happening in the first place.

In 2012, a medication called PrEP was developed. When taken daily, PrEP is very effective against HIV infection. Another treatment, PEP, when taken within three days of being exposed to HIV, can prevent HIV infection.

There are also treatments for HIV-positive pregnant women. If certain steps are followed, HIV will not pass from mother to child 99 percent of the time. For babies born with HIV, if treatment begins early, the virus can be controlled.

Today, we also know that HIV-positive people with undetectable levels of the virus cannot pass it on to others.

But what about a cure? Scientists continue to search.

In 2008 and 2017, two HIV-positive cancer patients were "cured" of their HIV after a bone-marrow transplant. This risky procedure wipes out a person's immune system, then replaces it using another person's stem cells. (Stem cells are the building blocks from which all other cells in the body are created.) Both patients received stem cells from someone with a natural immunity against catching HIV. (There are very few people in the world like this.)

The virus did not return in either patient, even after they stopped taking their HIV medications. (Doctors caution that the patients are not "cured"; they are "in remission," meaning the HIV is not there now but could come back.)

Then there is Loreen Willenberg. Loreen had been infected with HIV in 1992. However, her body had kept the virus from making her sick *without* the help of medicine. While the virus was always present in her body, it did not do her body harm. Then suddenly in 2020, researchers were unable to detect any HIV in Loreen's body at all. Loreen's body seemed to have cured *itself* of HIV infection!

Loreen is part of a study that includes sixty other people whose bodies also have been able to stop the virus. Researchers want to learn how these people's bodies naturally prevent HIV from making them sick.

Loreen Willenberg

Advances in science and technology since the 1980s have led to incredible discoveries. People look forward to the coming years and what new research will bring. There is a great sense of hope and possibility that the first PWAs could only have dreamed of.

CHAPTER 11
The Crisis at Hand

With deaths from AIDS and new cases of HIV on the decline worldwide, one might think that the AIDS crisis is over. But that is certainly not the case.

In 2019, there were 38 million people living with HIV/AIDS worldwide. Of these, 26 million were receiving treatment, but an estimated seven million were unaware they even had it, and thus could be spreading HIV to others. Hundreds of thousands still die every year, and in 2019, there were as many as two million new cases of HIV. In some countries, HIV/AIDS still kills more people than any other disease.

In the United States, progress has begun to stall. In 2014, there were around 38,000 new cases reported; by 2018, the number was the same. In fact, cases have increased in the South. The state of Florida is home to half of all HIV-positive Americans.

Communities of color and low-income Americans are affected at higher rates. Though the United States' population is roughly 14 percent Black, nearly half of Americans living with HIV/AIDS are Black. Almost one in four is Hispanic/Latinx. This is not fair. It happens because getting proper health care and medications is out of reach for many people. HIV meds can cost over fifty dollars a day.

As survivors of HIV/AIDS approach old age, many have health problems after taking so many medications for so many years. AIDS survivors are at greater risk for cancer, heart disease, and organ failure. Many experience depression, having lost so many loved ones to the disease. Some have feelings of terrible guilt for having survived, when so many others did not.

Film historian Vito Russo, speaking at the state capitol in Albany, New York, in 1988, said:

"Someday, the AIDS crisis will be over. . . . And when that day comes . . . there will be people . . . who will hear the story that once there was a terrible disease . . . and that a brave group of people stood up and fought and . . . gave their lives, so that other people might live and be free."

Until that day comes, the work continues.

Timeline of the AIDS Crisis

1908	HIV transmitted from chimpanzee to human in Africa
1967	HIV/AIDS reaches Haiti, and the United States soon after
1970–1976	Virus begins spreading rapidly within the gay community, first in New York, then in San Francisco
1980	Gay men begin dying of AIDS-related illness
1981	CDC publishes its first report on HIV/AIDS in June
	In August, Larry Kramer raises $6,635 for research
1982	GMHC (Gay Men's Health Crisis) founded in January
	CDC reports HIV/AIDS spread through sexual contact
1983	People with AIDS (PWA) founded in Denver, Colorado
	First AIDS ward opens at San Francisco General Hospital
1985	First HIV tests developed
	Rock Hudson announces AIDS diagnosis
	Ryan White refused admittance to his school
1987	ACT UP founded in March
	AIDS Memorial Quilt unveiled in October
	AZT hits the market at an annual cost of $10,000
1995	Combination drug therapy ("the cocktail") first available
2012	PrEP, a daily treatment to prevent HIV, becomes available
2020	Loreen Willenberg "cures herself" of HIV, giving hope that researchers may one day discover a cure

Timeline of the World

1908	Ford Motor Company produces the Model T automobile
1967	Aretha Franklin's song "Respect" tops the pop charts
1969	Police raid the Stonewall Inn, a gay bar in New York City, on June 28, accelerating a queer-rights movement
1976	Apple Computer founded
1980	US men's hockey team defeats the Soviet team at the Winter Olympics
1981	Royal wedding of Prince Charles and Lady Diana Spencer
1982	*Time* magazine names "The Computer" Man of the Year
1983	Nintendo launches Mario Bros. arcade game in Japan
1984	MTV airs first annual Video Music Awards show
1985	Wreckage of the *Titanic* located in the North Atlantic
1987	*Star Trek: The Next Generation* series premieres on CBS
1995	*Toy Story*, the first fully computer-animated feature film, is released
2006	Twitter is launched, and by 2021, it will have more than 350 million users
2012	President Barack Obama becomes the first sitting US president to support same-sex marriage
2019	COVID-19 begins to spread worldwide
2020	Vaccines to protect against COVID-19 developed

Bibliography

*Books for young readers

*Alsenas, Linas. *Gay America: Struggle for Equality*. New York: Amulet Books, 2008.

*Bausum, Ann. *Stonewall: Breaking Out in the Fight for Gay Rights*. New York: Viking, 2015.

*Bausum, Ann. *Viral: The Fight Against AIDS in America*. New York: Viking, 2019.

France, David, director. *How to Survive a Plague*. IFC Films, 2012.

*Medina, Nico. *What Was Stonewall?* New York: Penguin Workshop, 2019.

Shilts, Randy. *And the Band Played On: Politics, People, and the AIDS Epidemic*. New York: St. Martin's Press, 1987.

Weissman, David, director. *We Were Here*. Weissman Projects LLC, 2011.